THIS BOOK

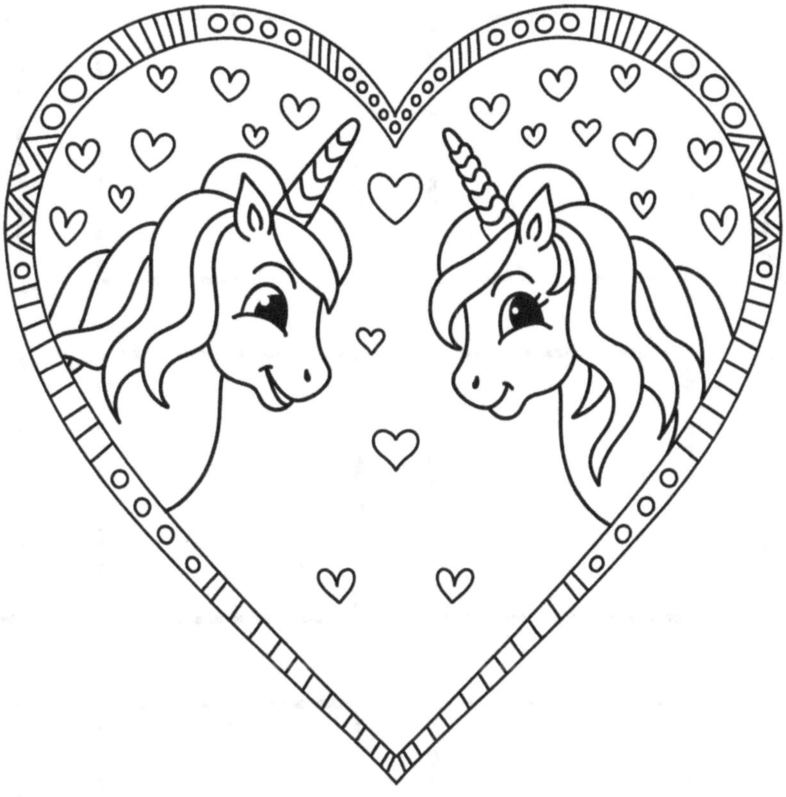

BELONGS TO

COLOR TEST

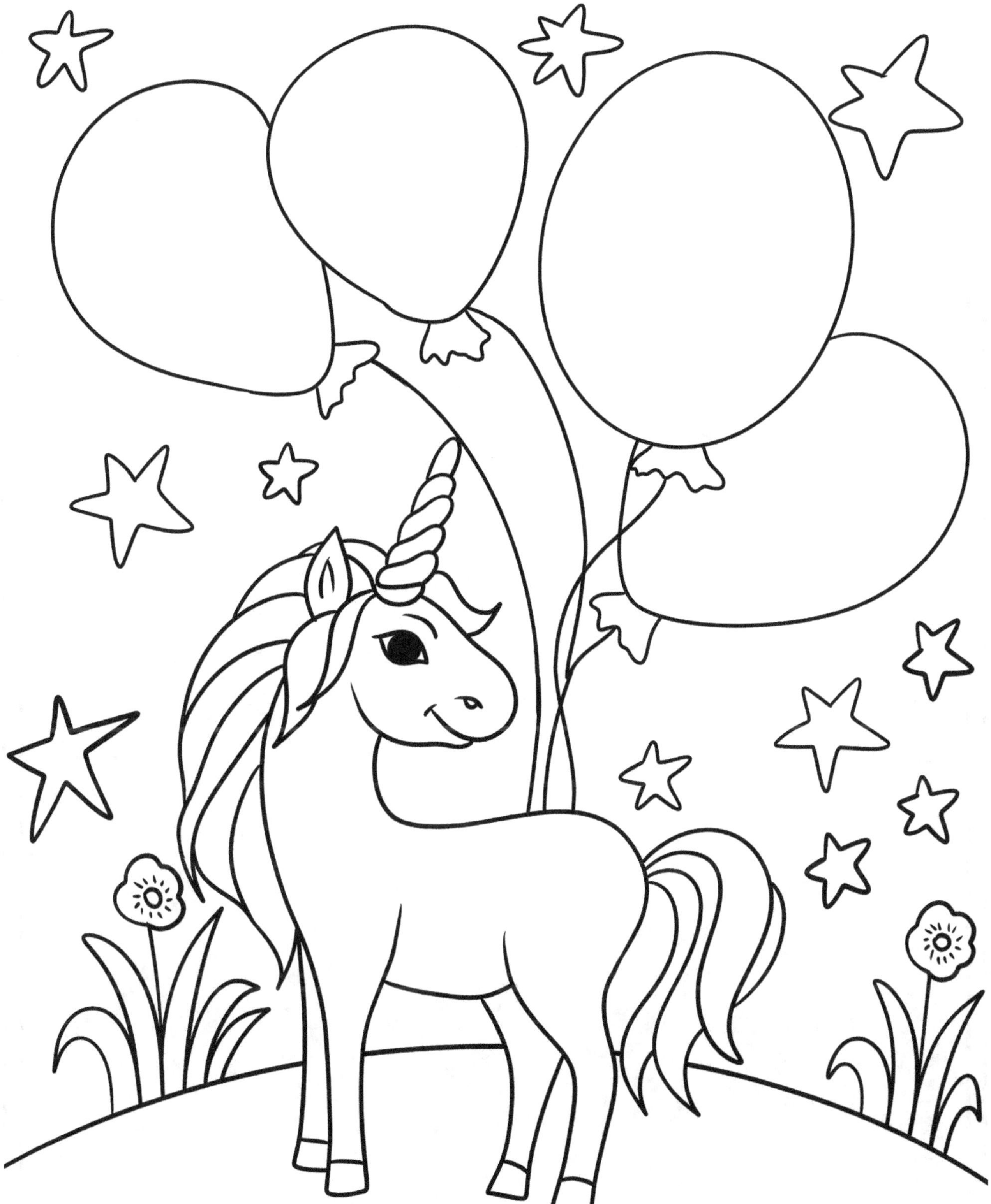

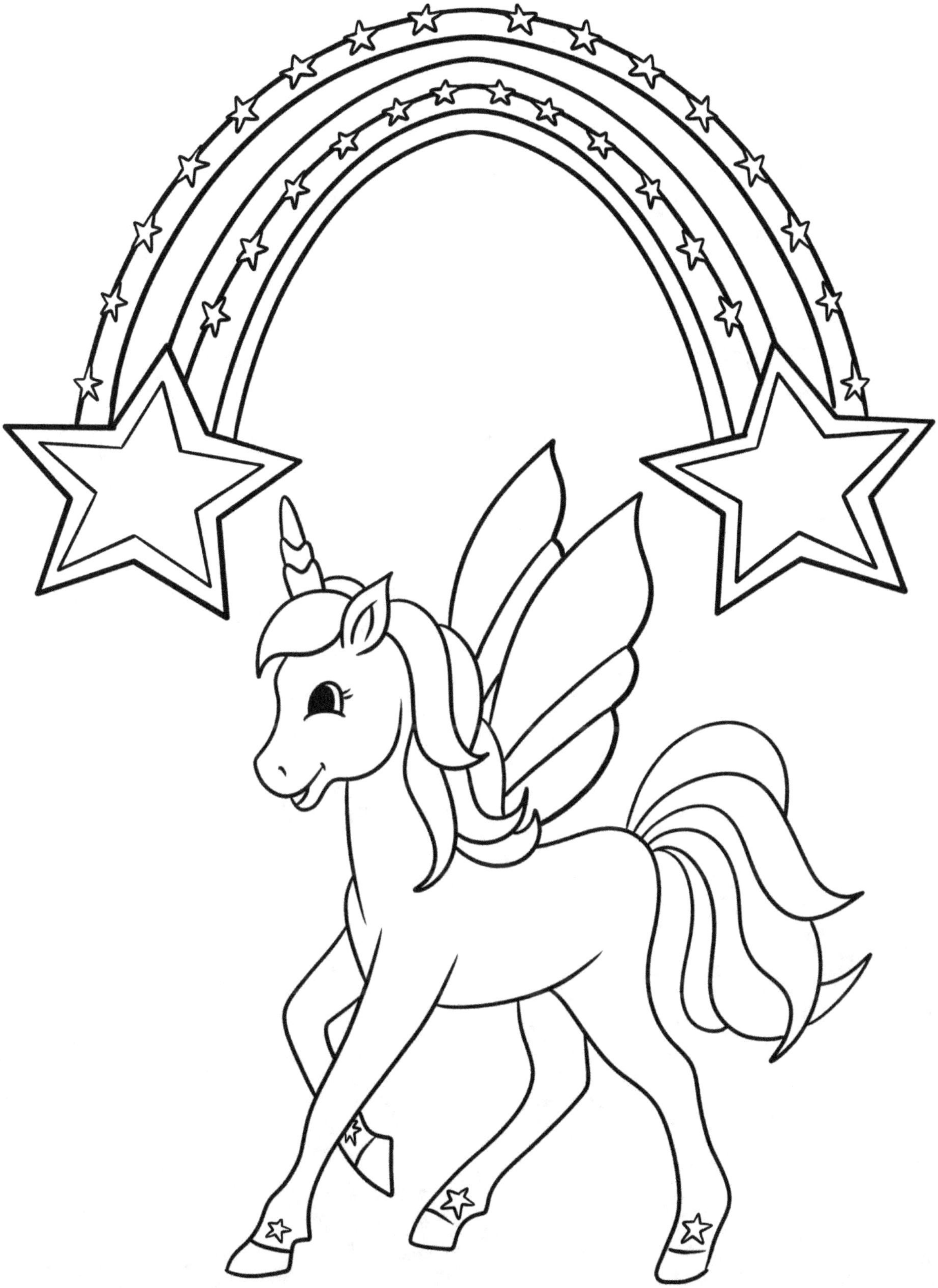

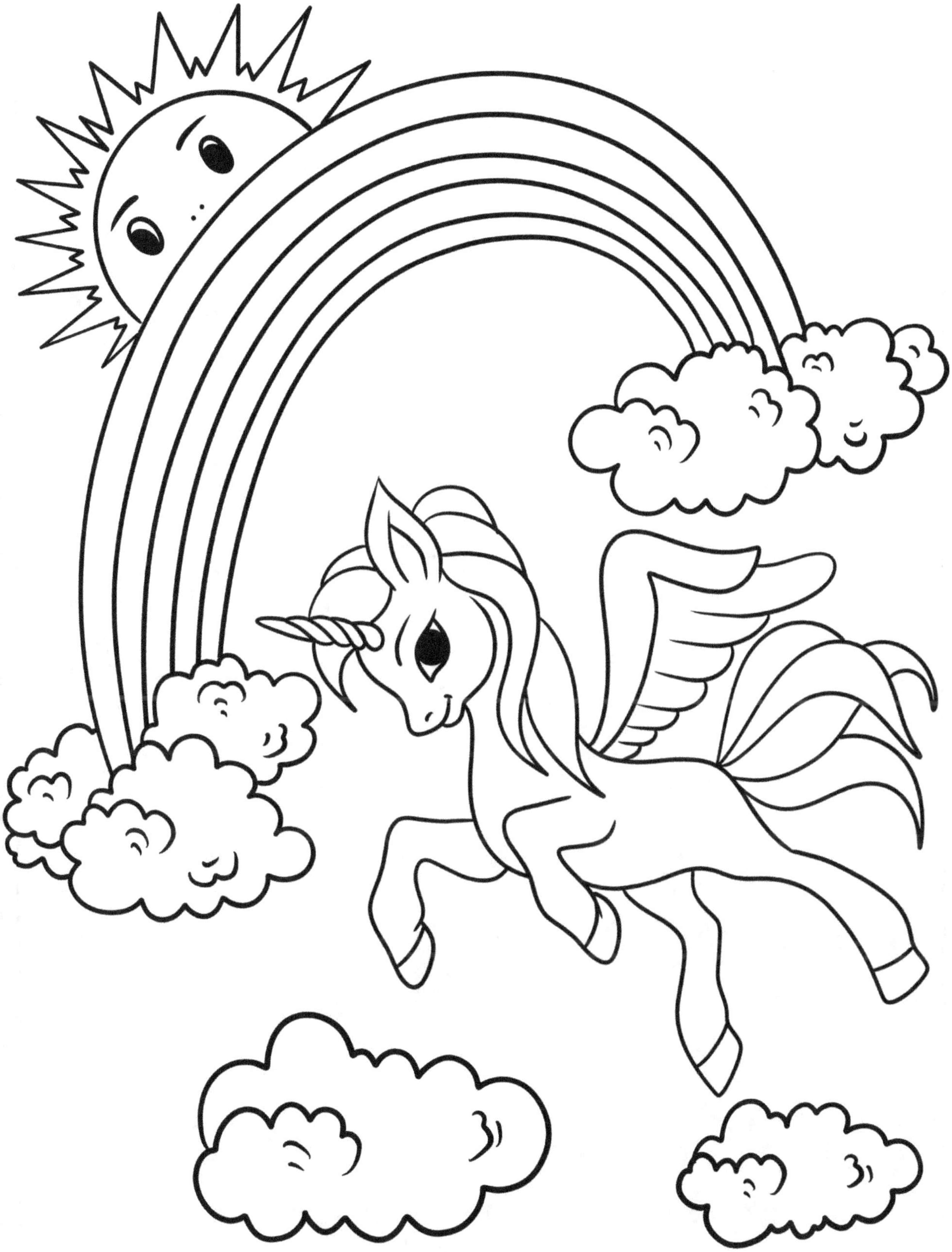

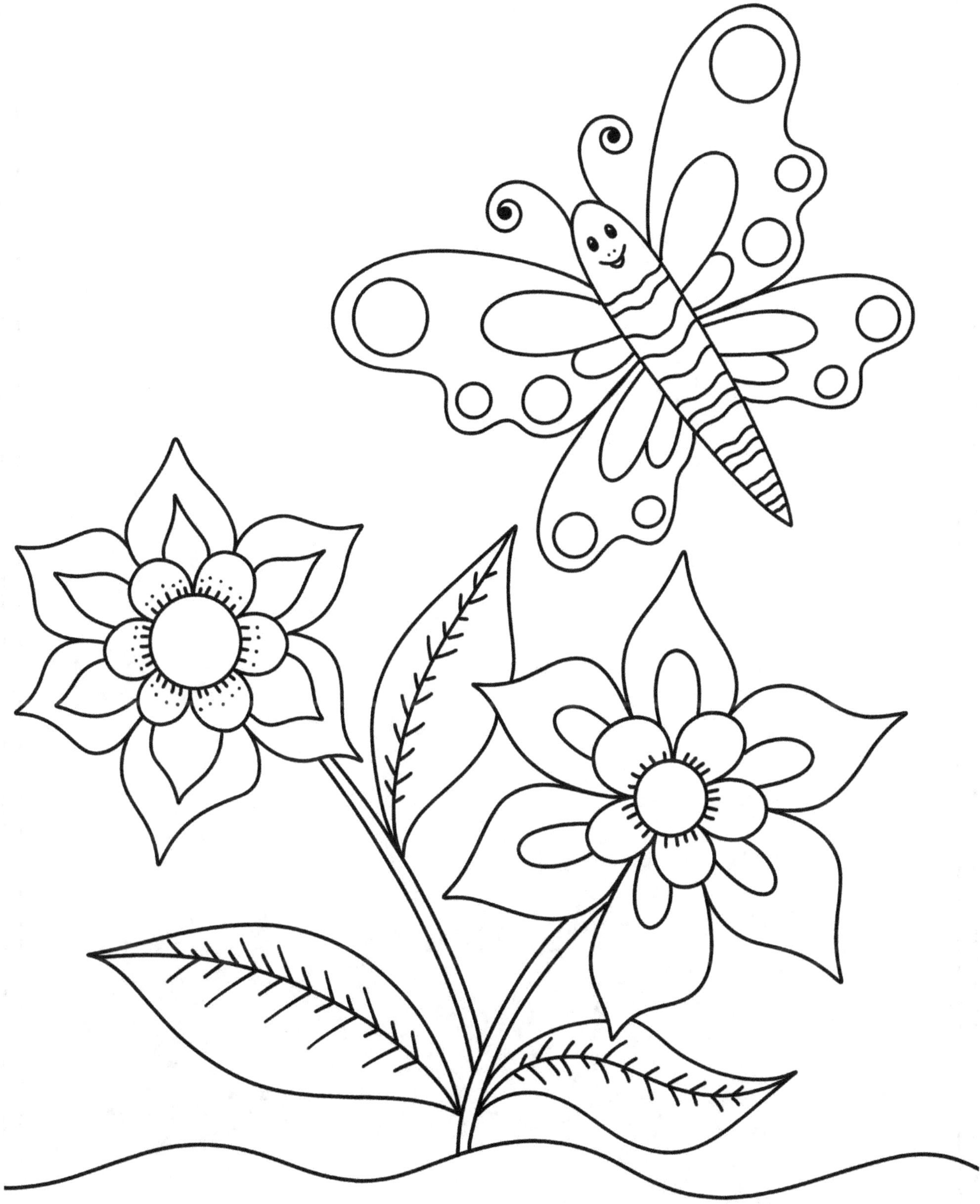

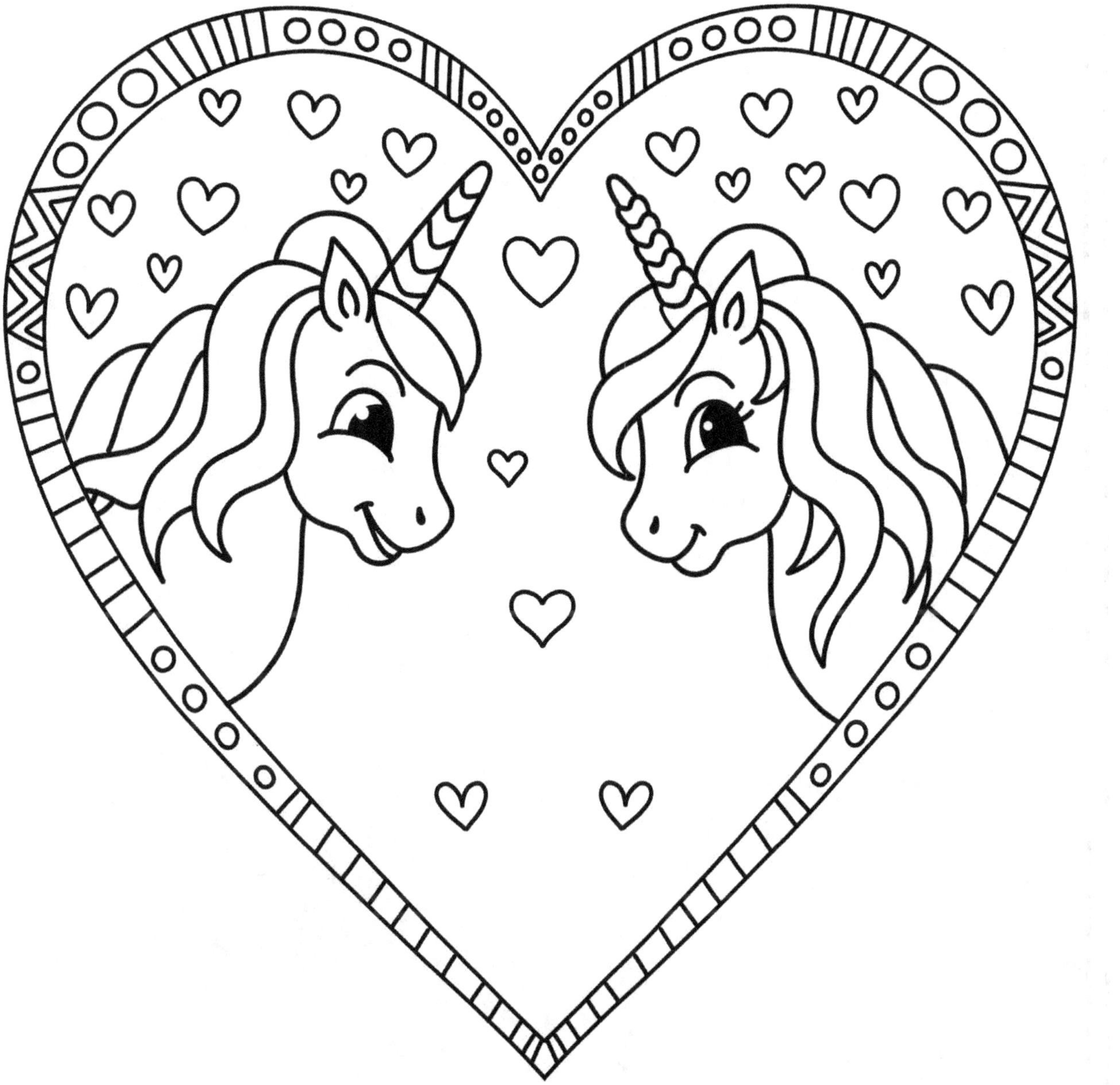

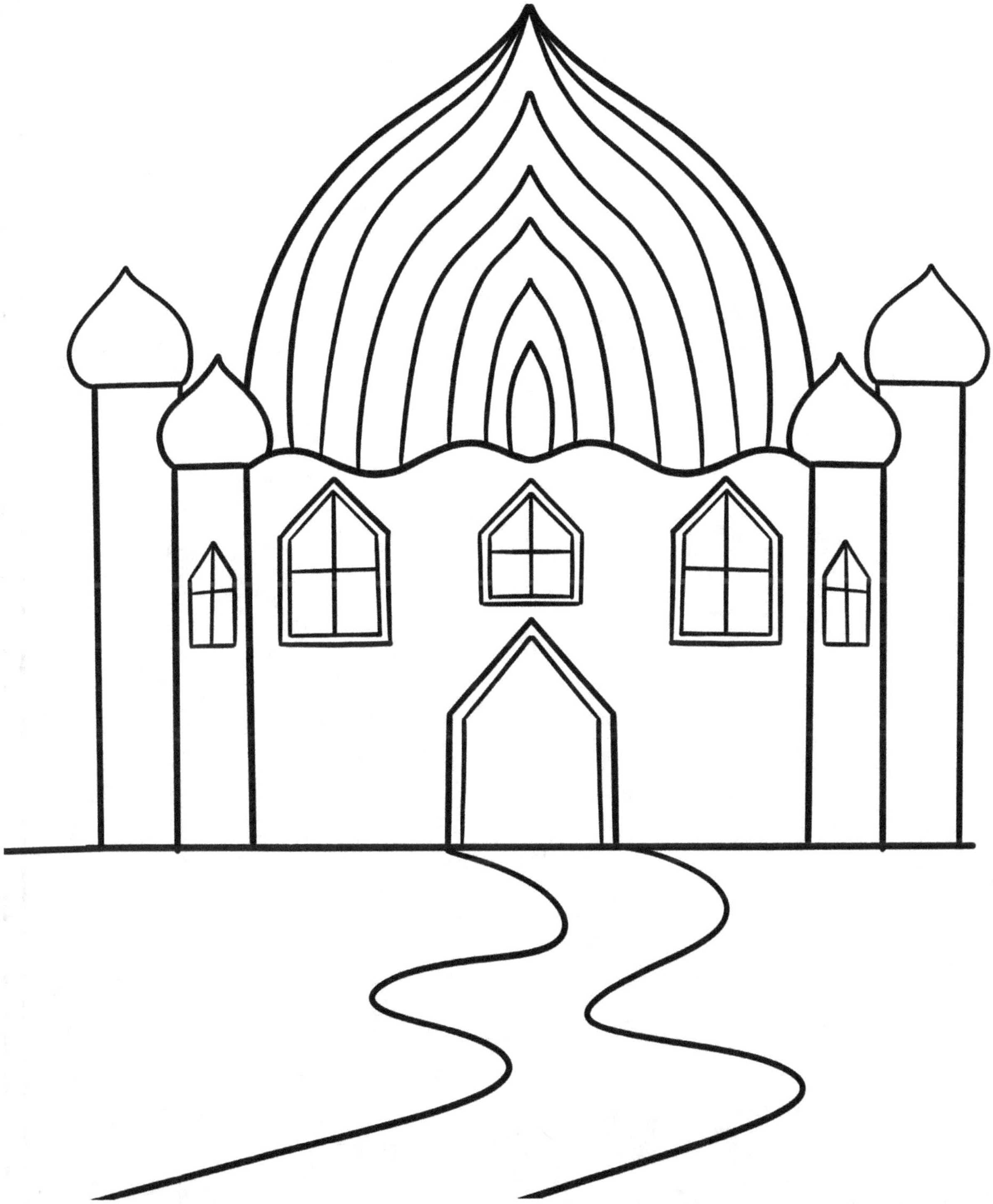

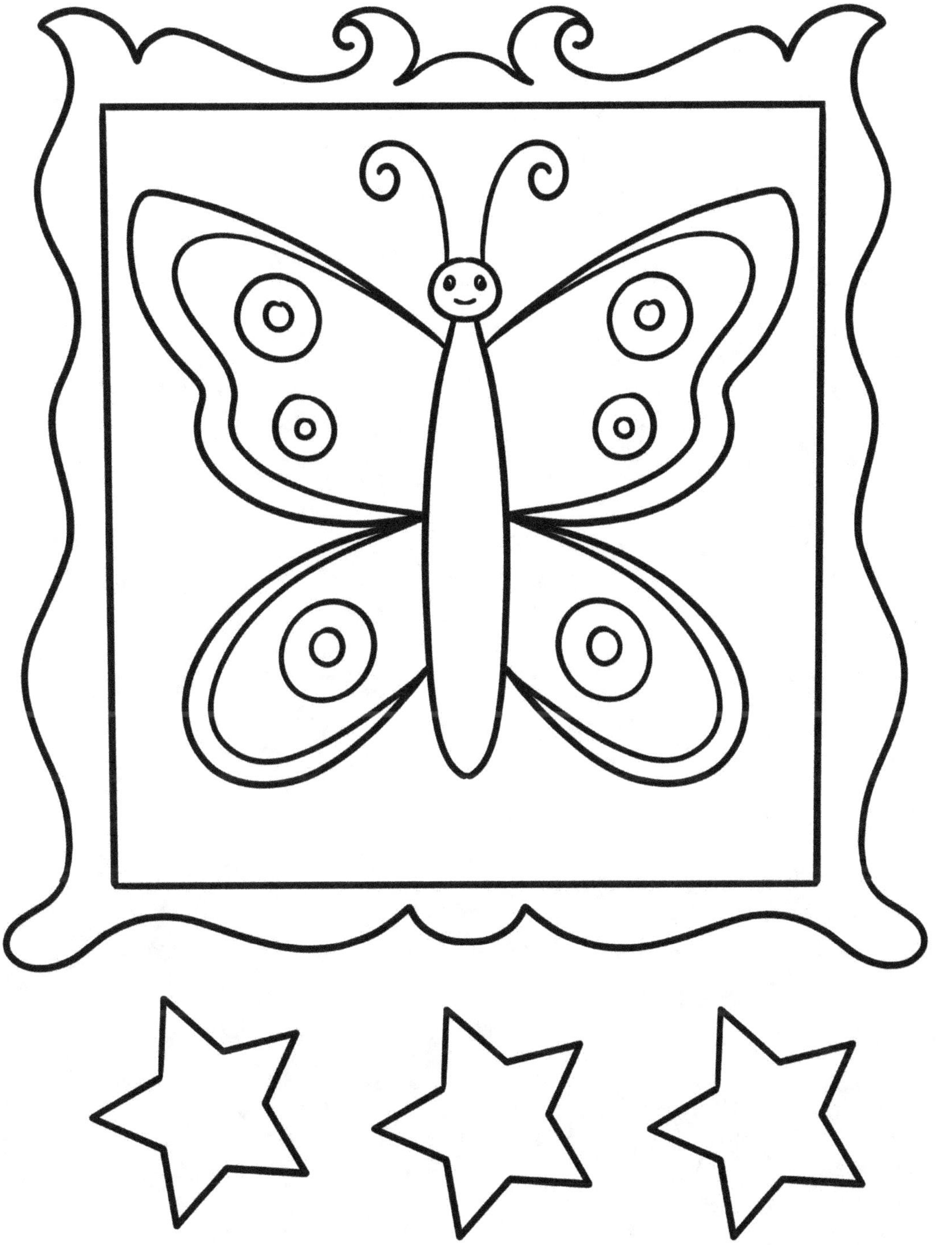

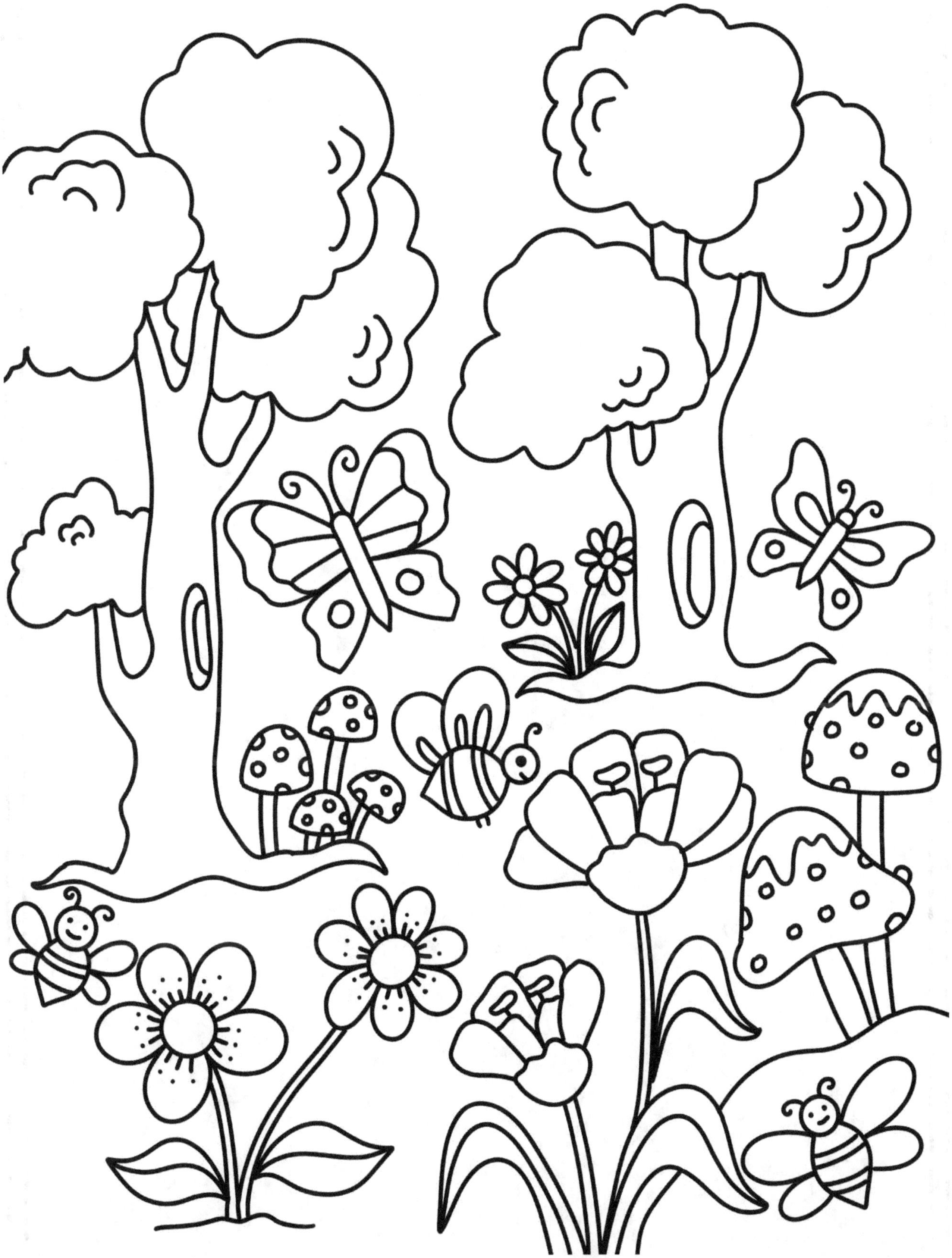

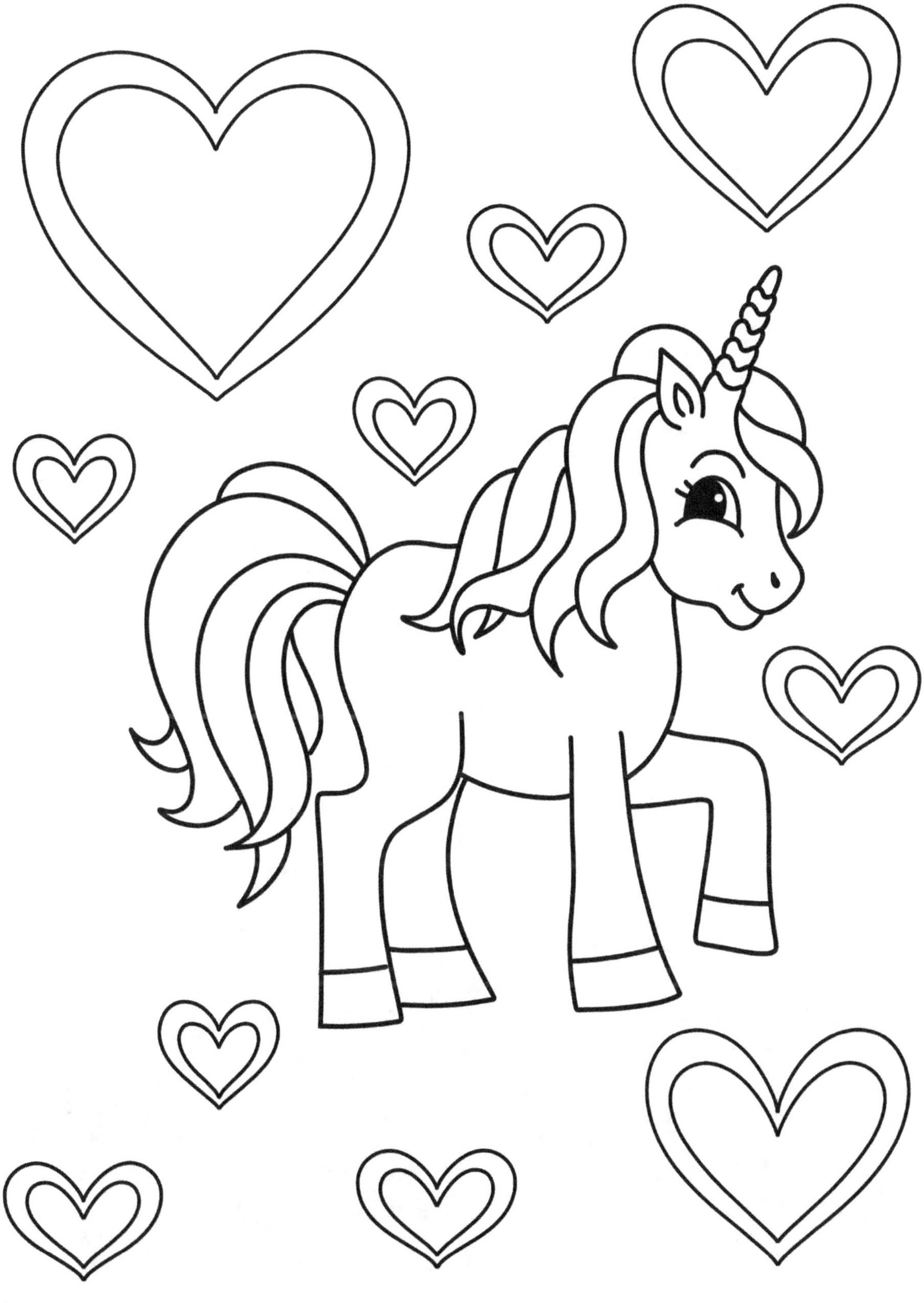

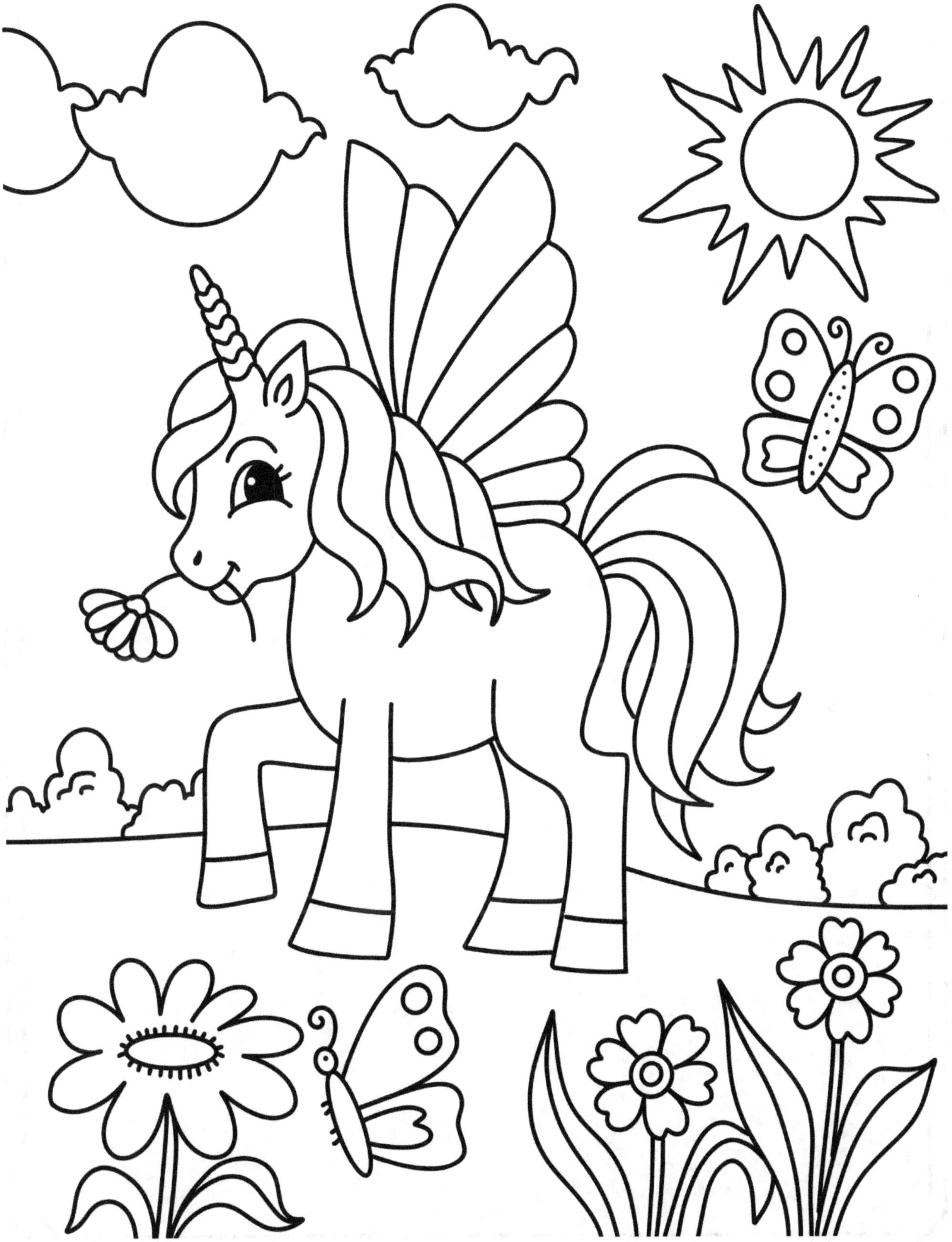

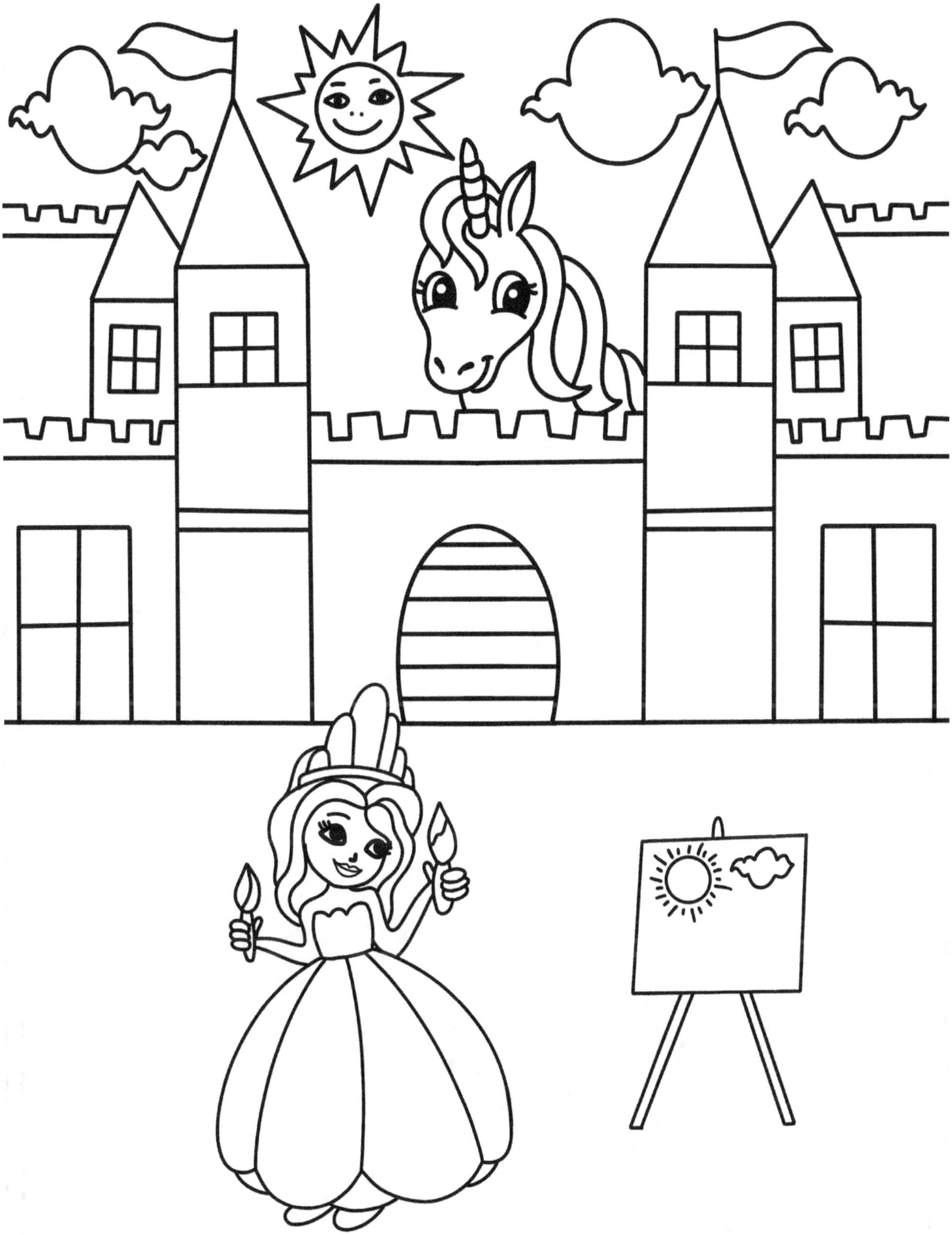

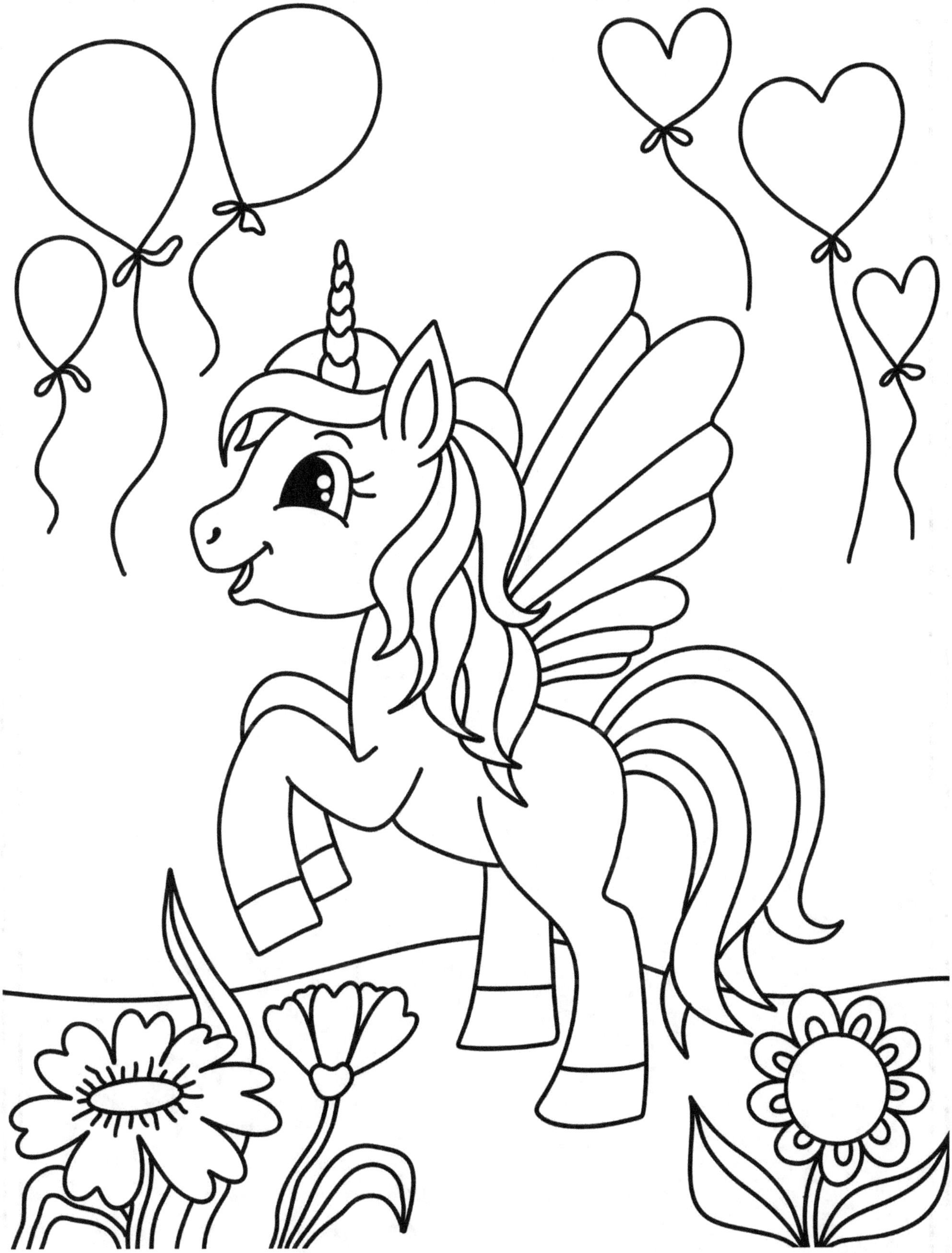

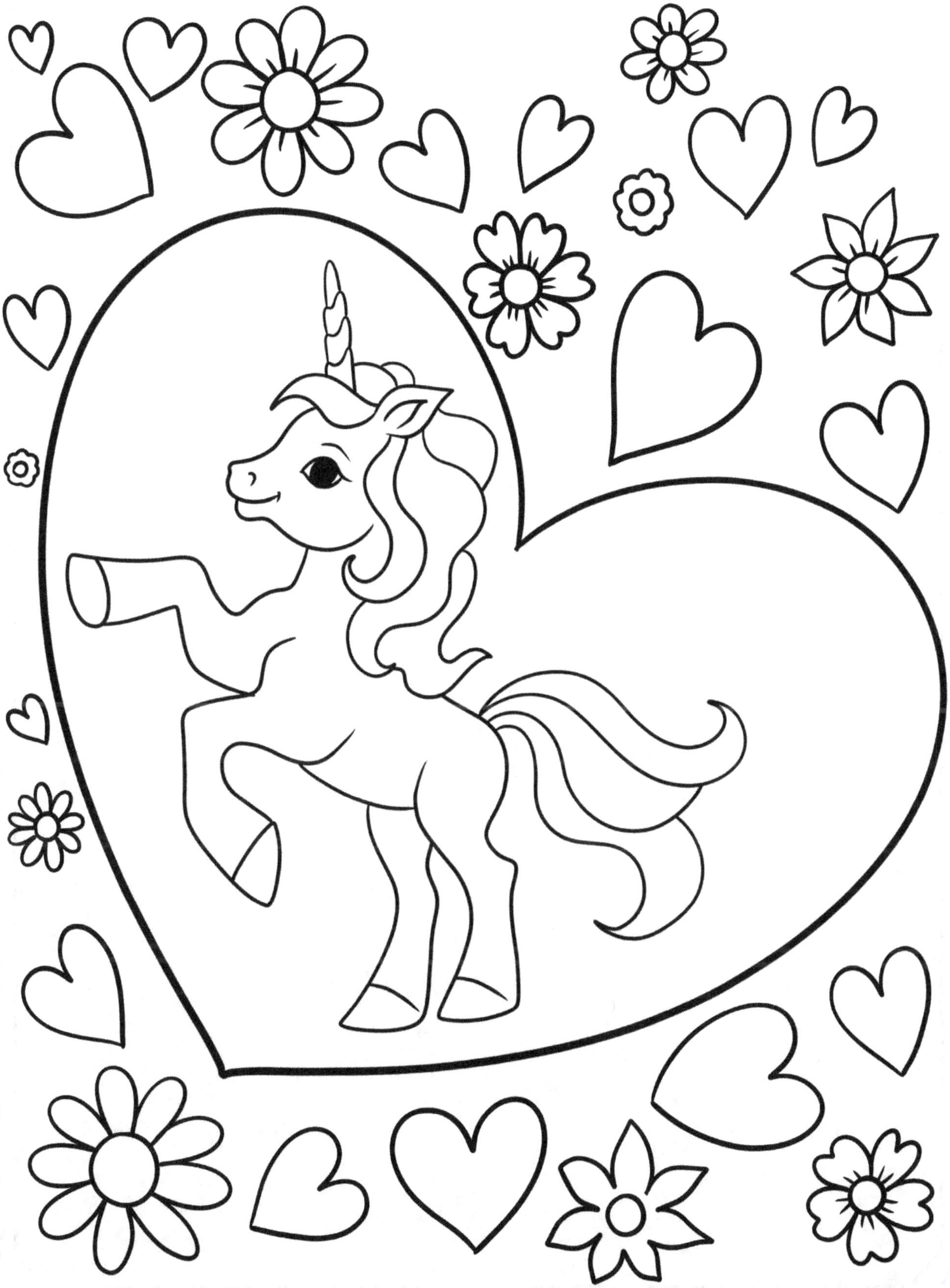

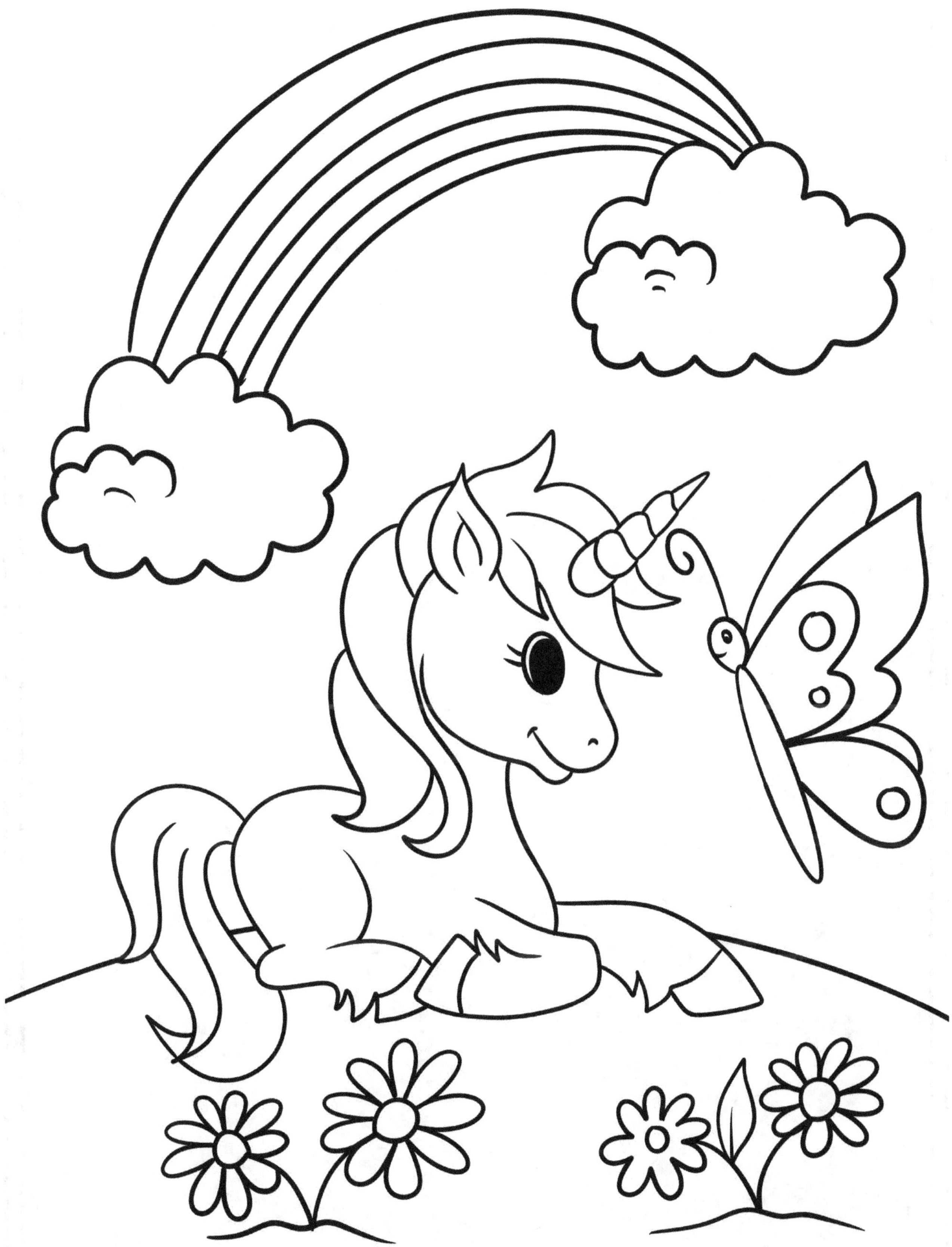

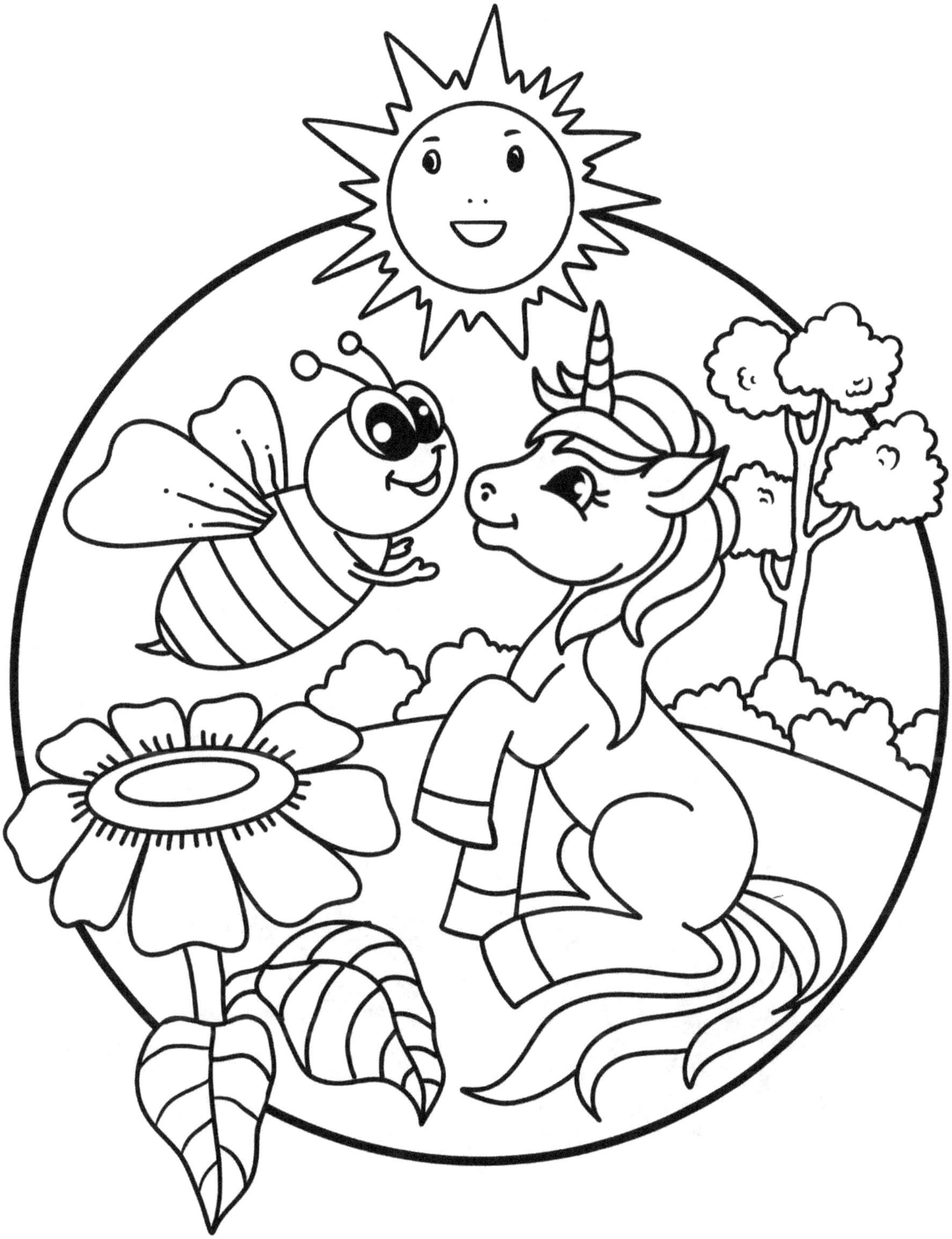

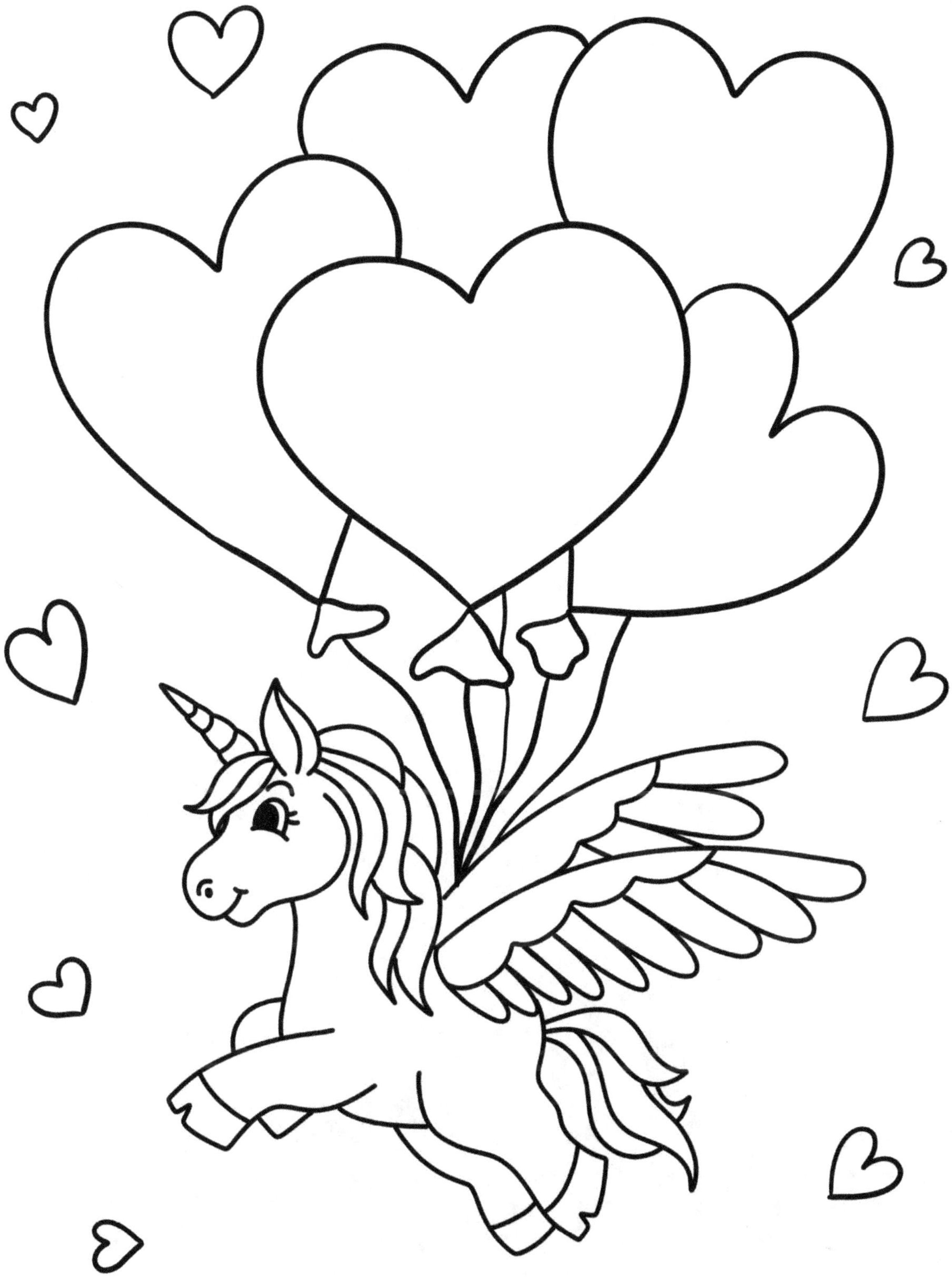

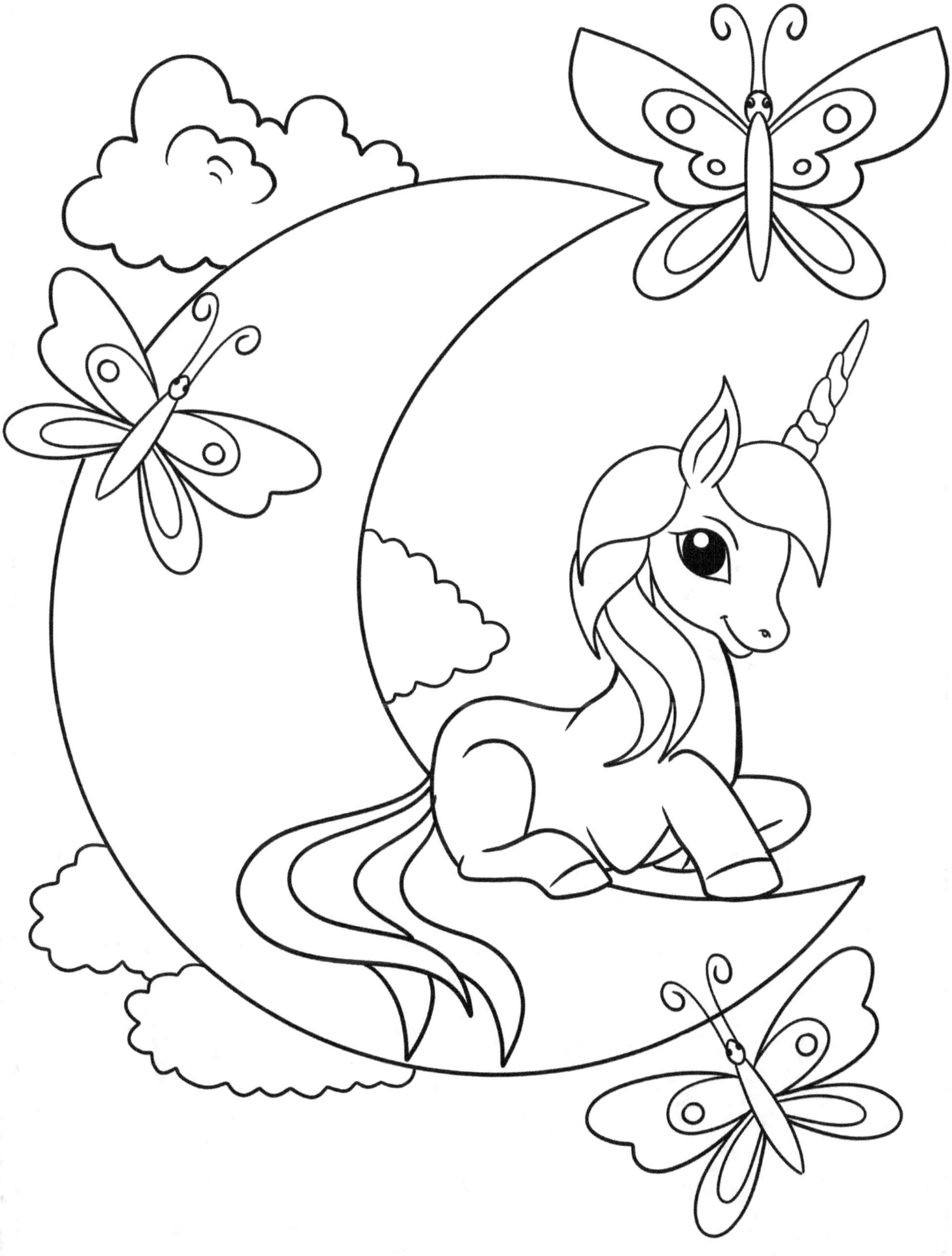

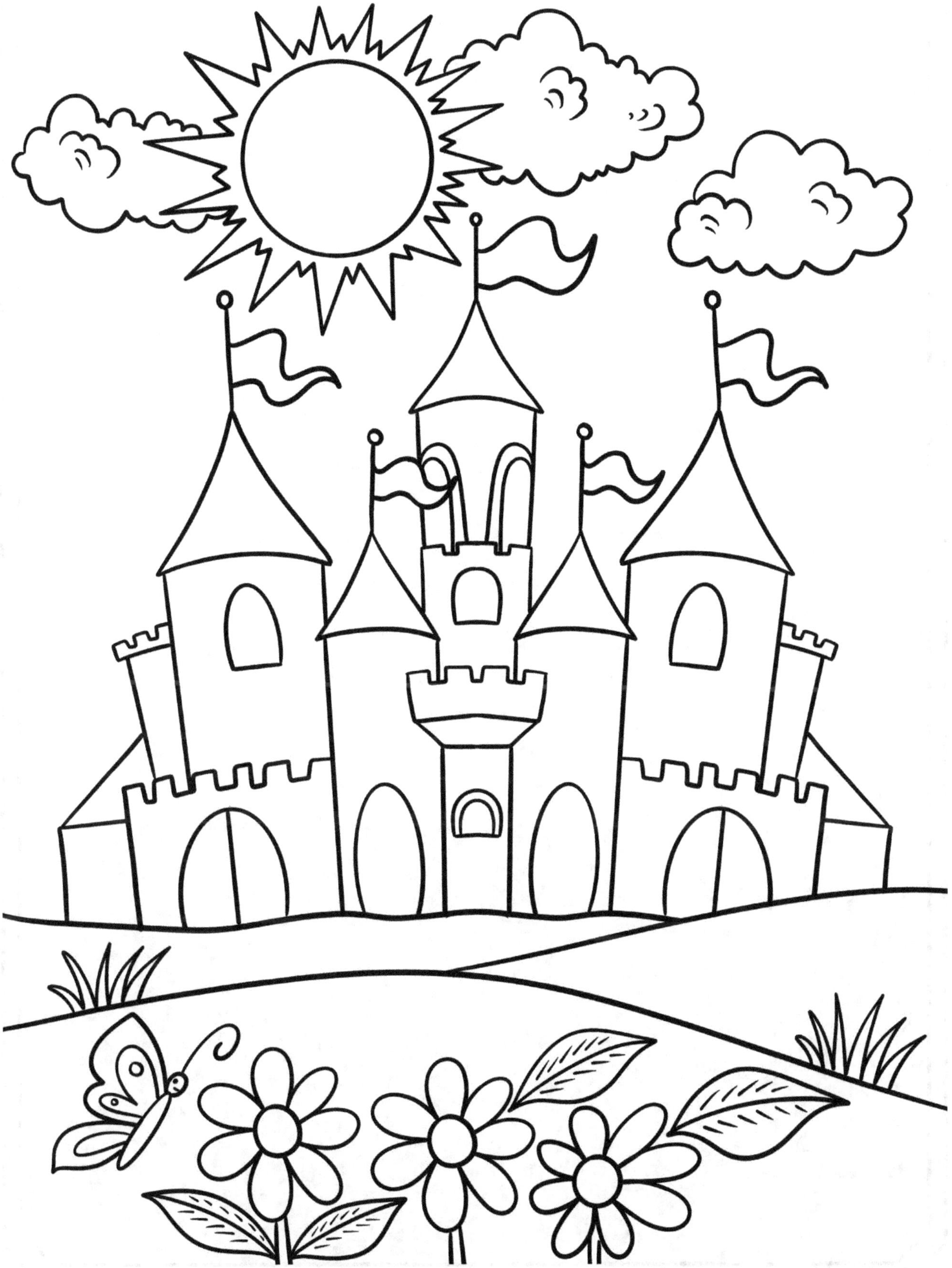

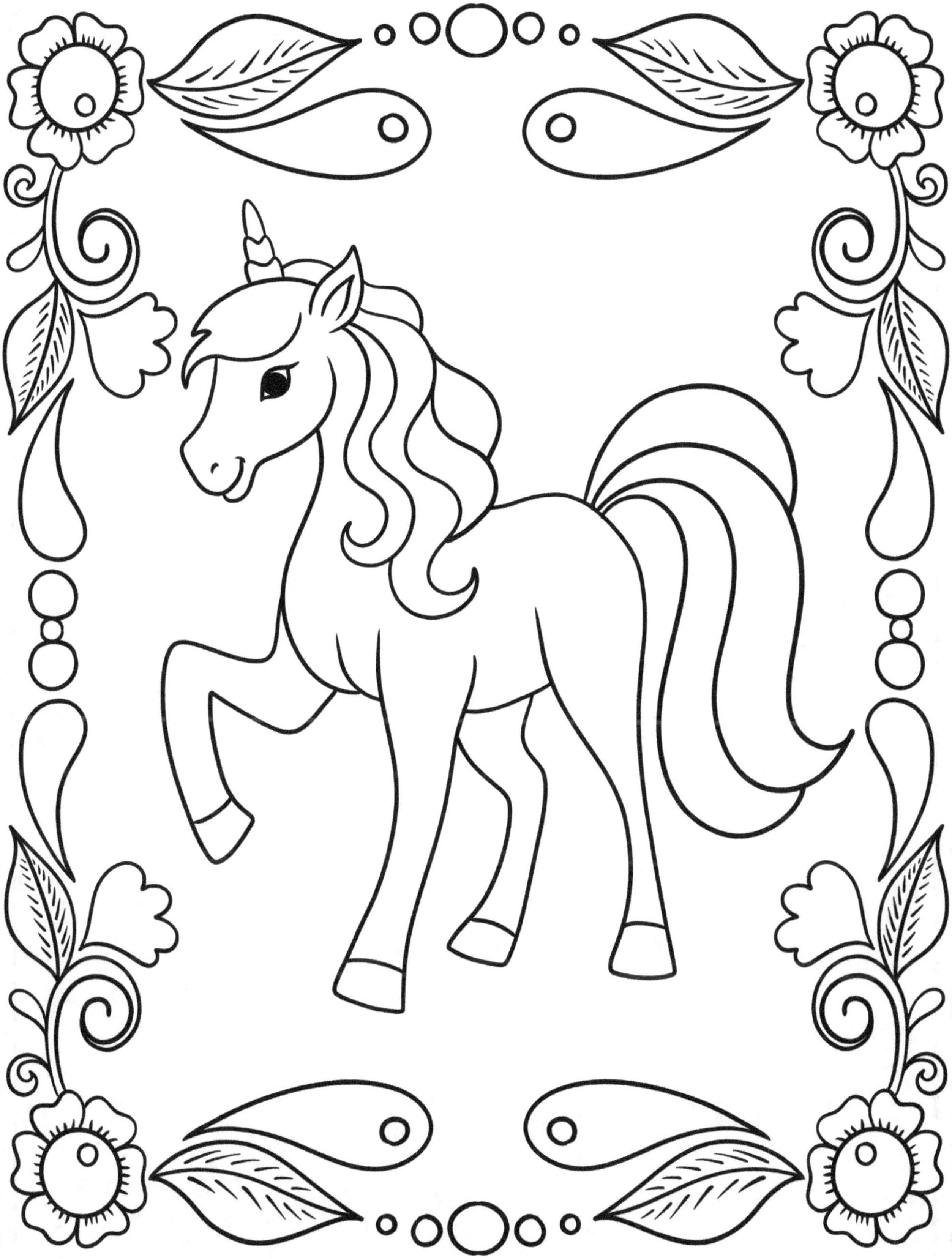

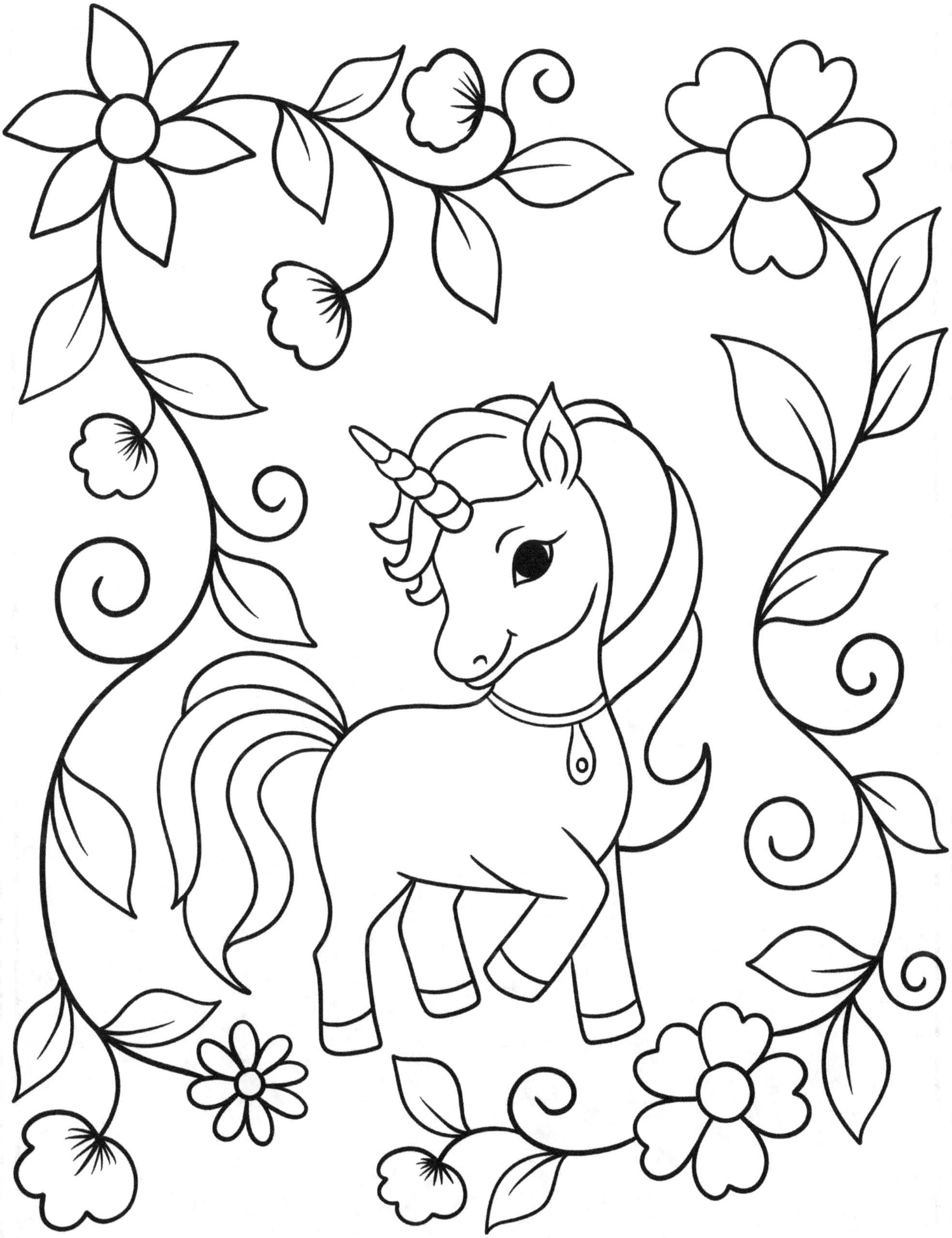

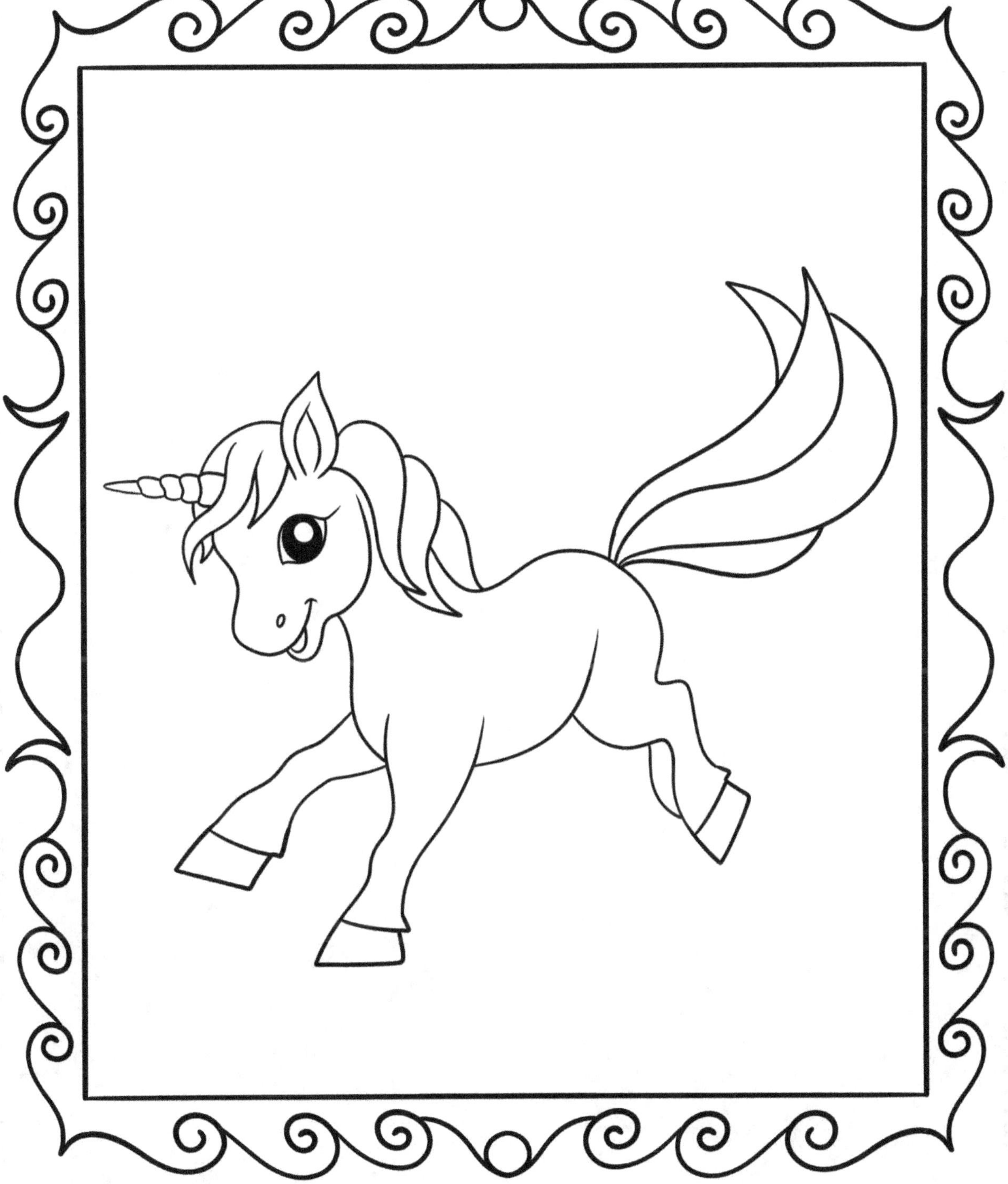

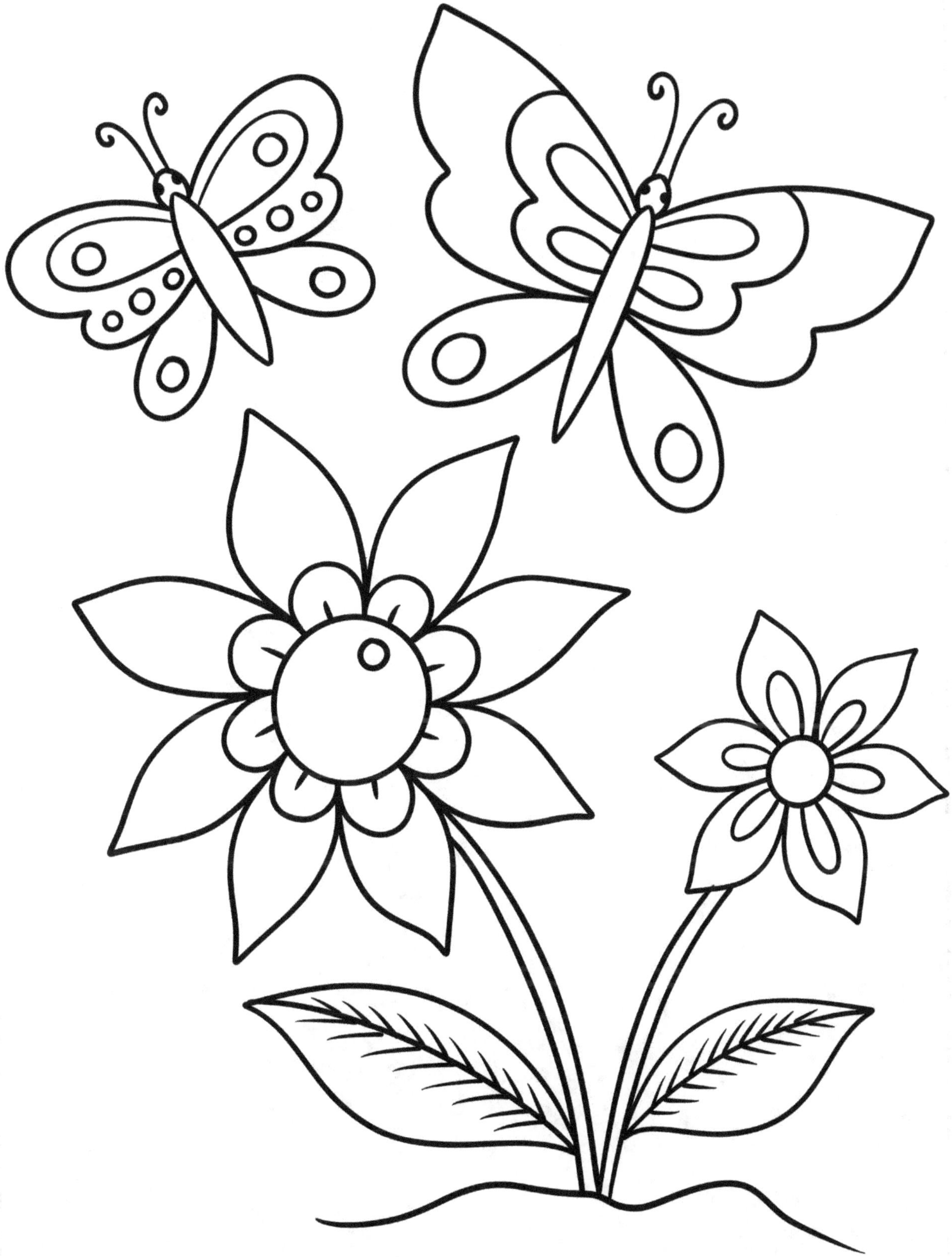

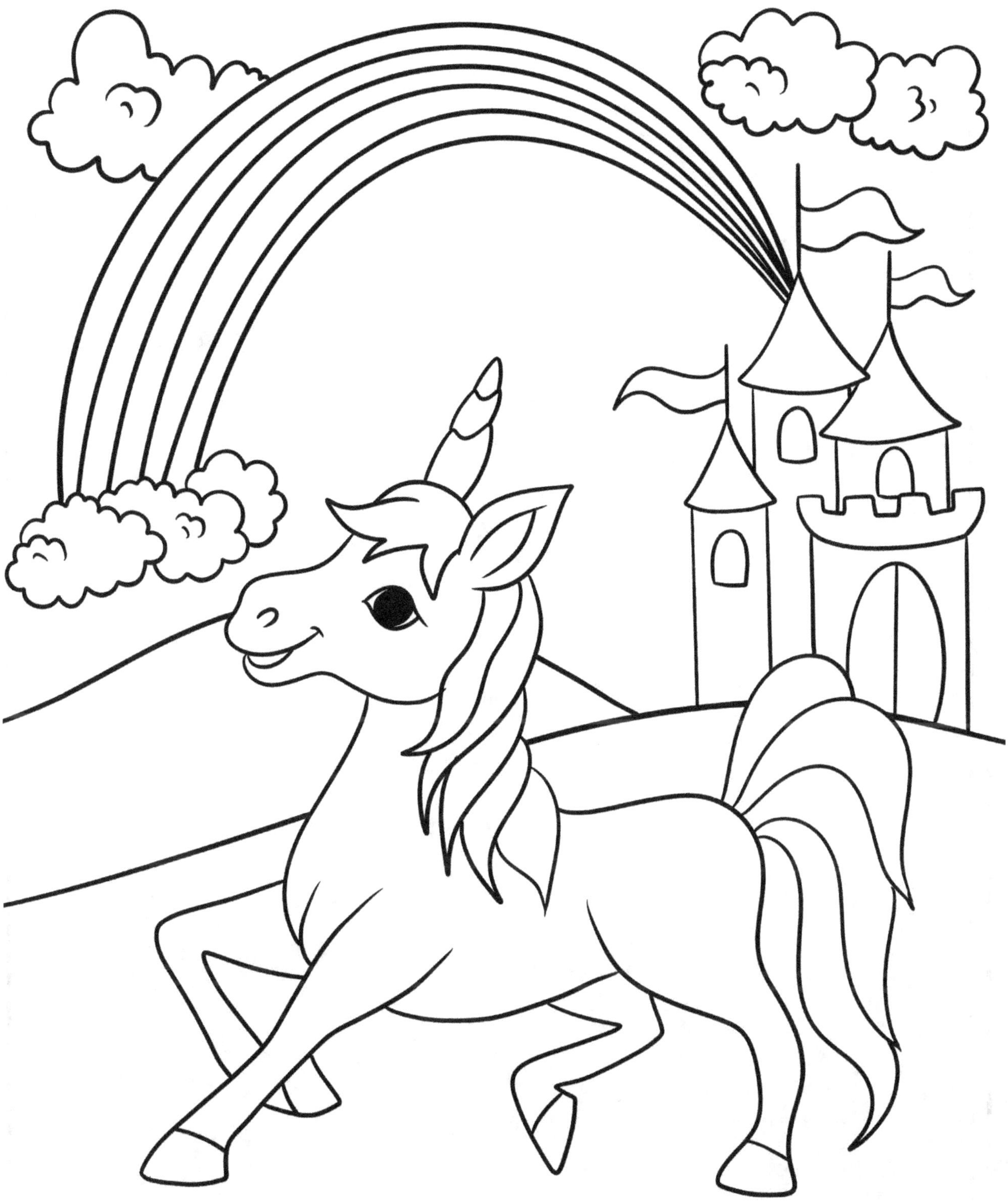

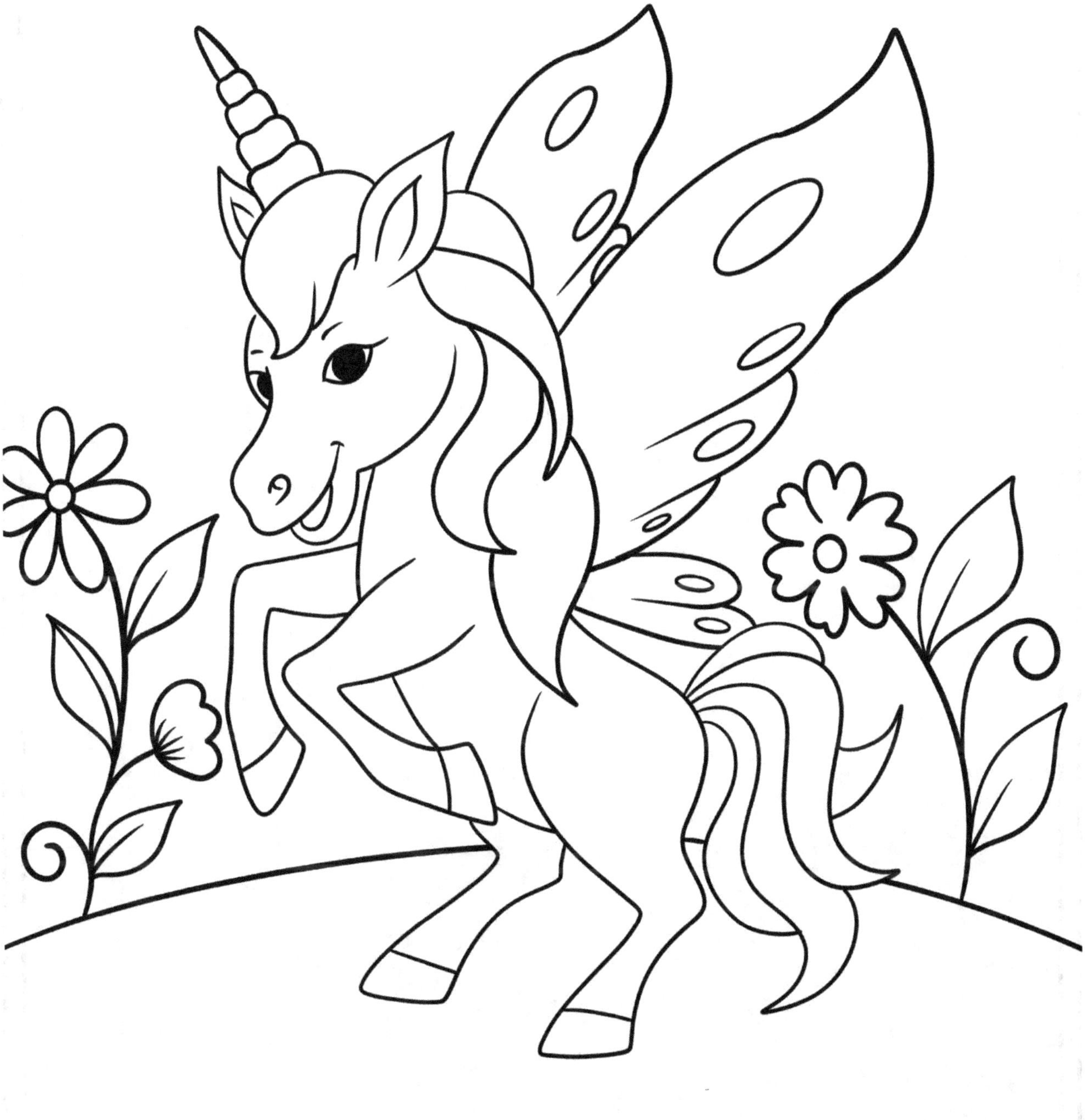

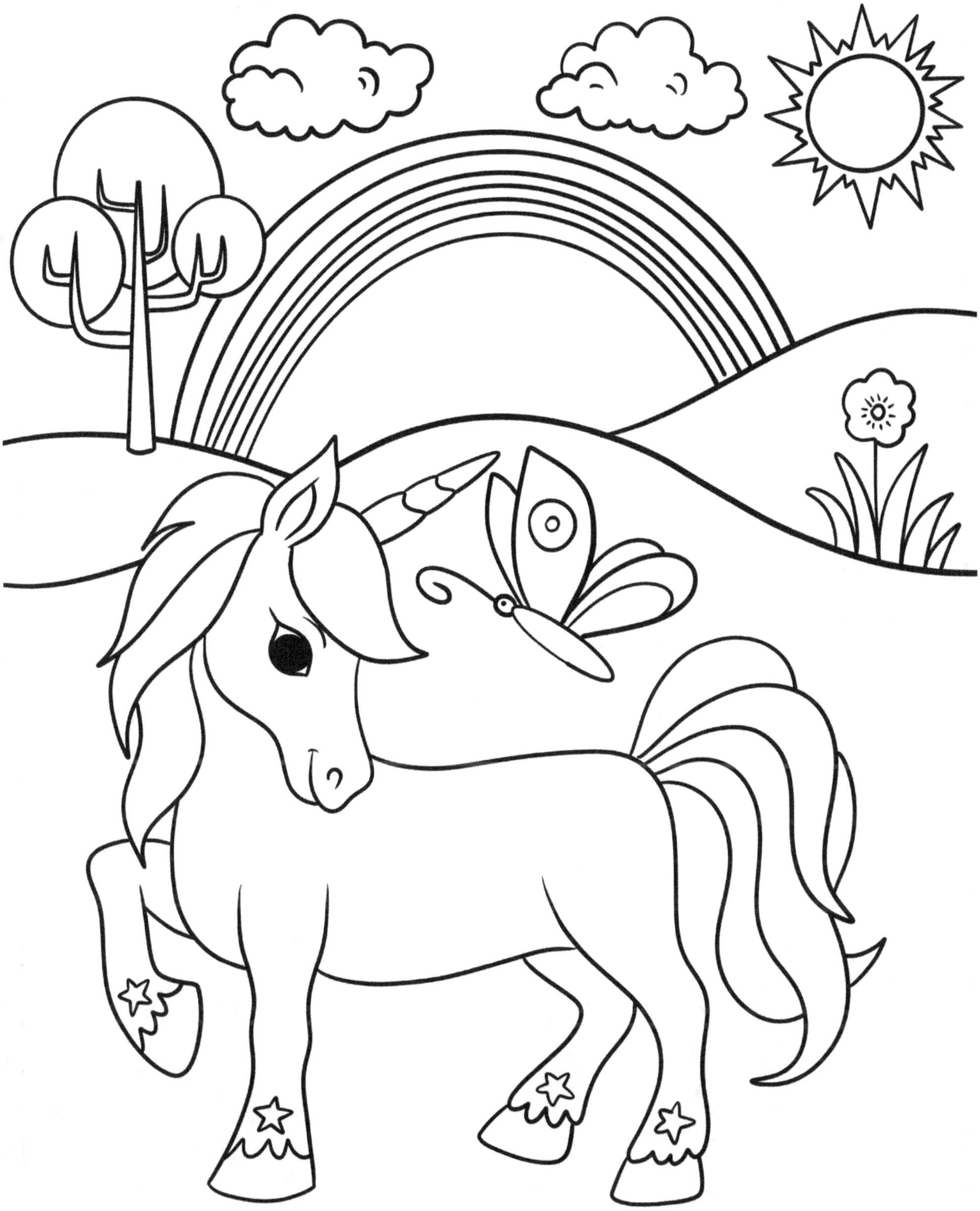

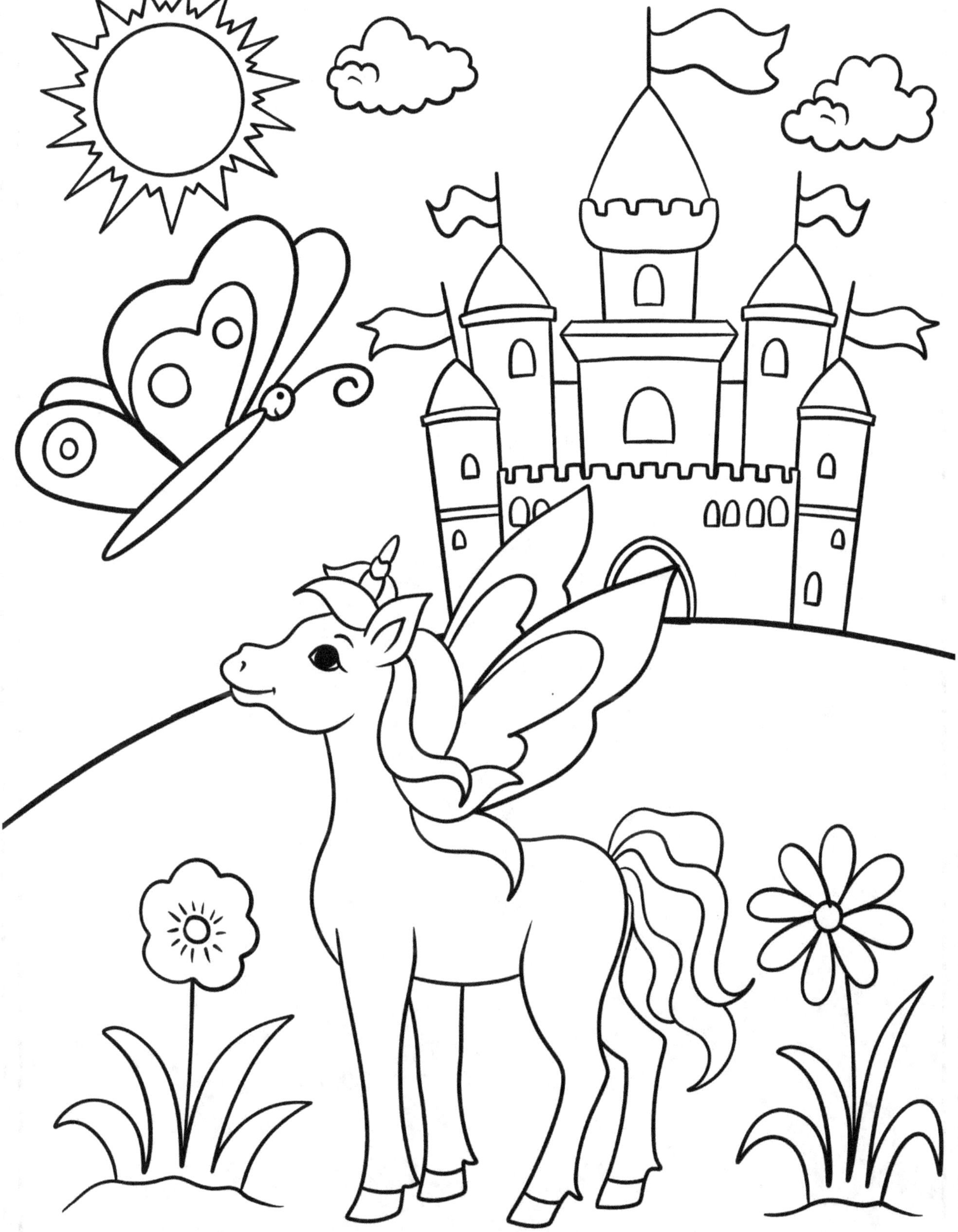

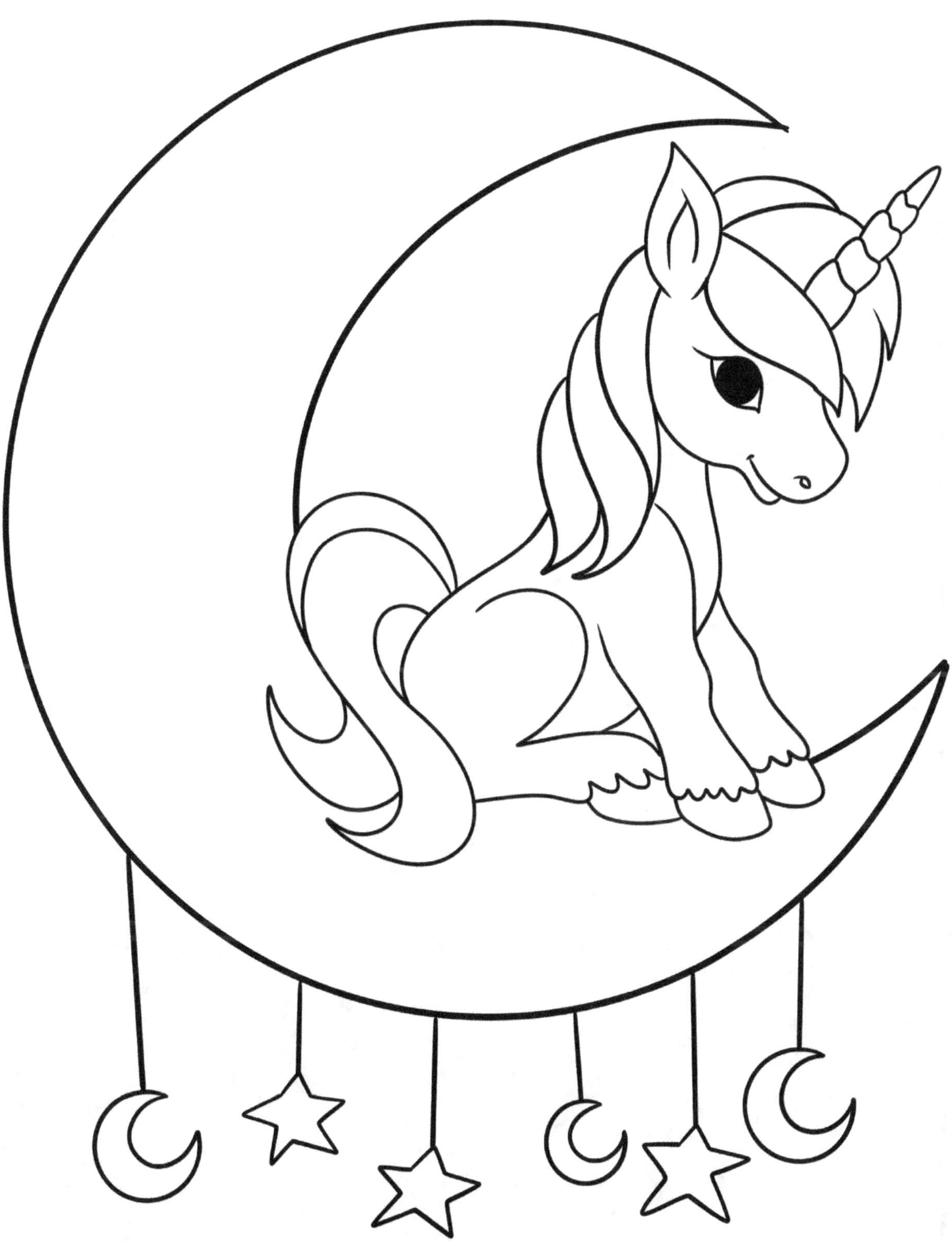

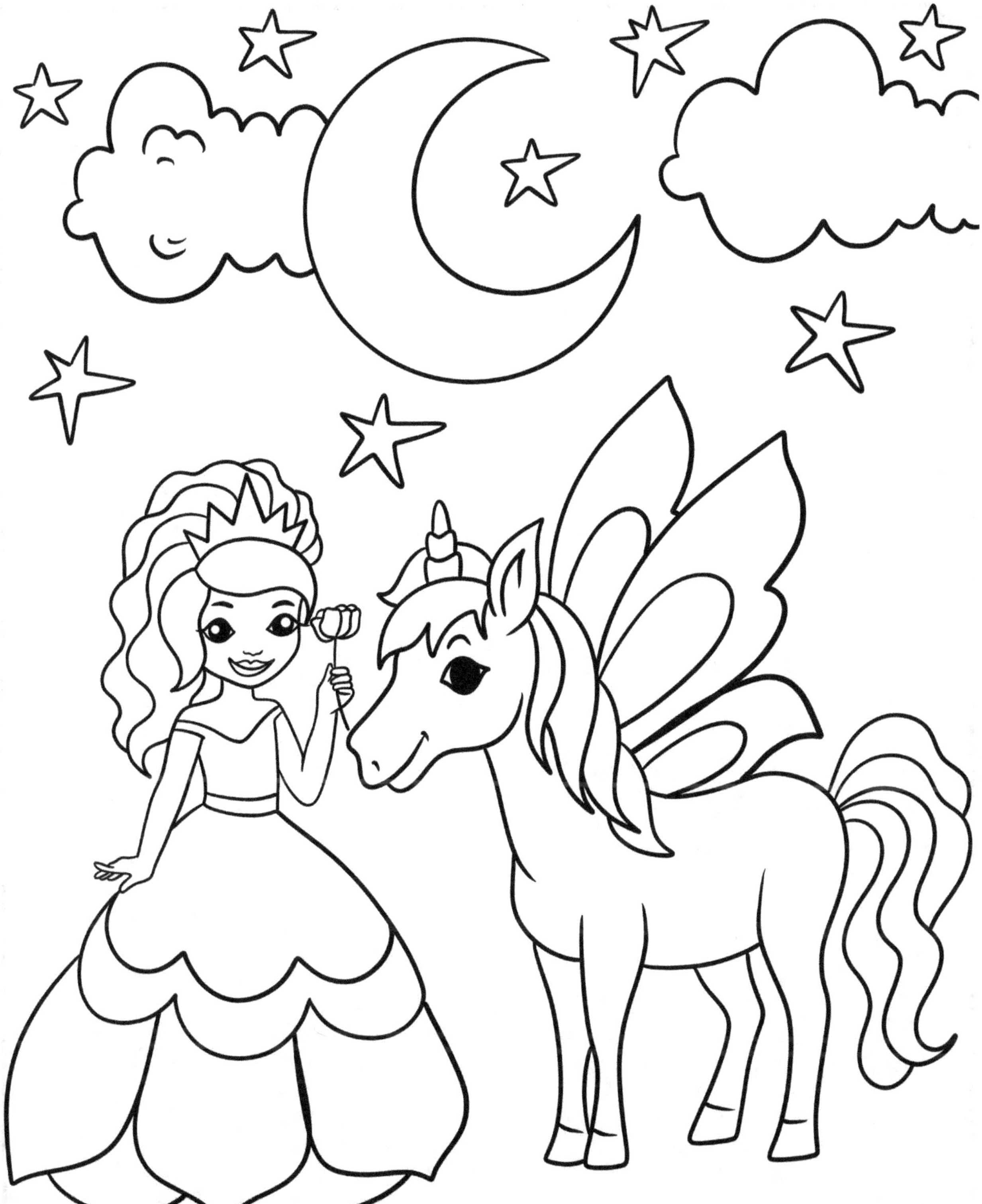

www.ingramcontent.com/pod-product-compliance
Lightning Source LLC
Chambersburg PA
CBHW080530220526
45465CB00006B/2657
9798664402063